Trains & Things!
A Kid's Guide To Carson City, Nevada

Photography by John D. Weigand
Poetry by Penelope Dyan

Bellissima Publishing, LLC
Jamul, California
www.bellissimapublishing.com

Copyright © 2015 by Penny D. Weigand and John D. Weigand

All rights reserved. No part of this book may be reproduced or transmitted in any form or by any means, electronic or mechanical, including photocopying, recording, or by any other means, or by any information or storage retrieval system, without permission from the publisher.

ISBN 978-1-61477-188-3
First Edition

"Life must be lived as play."

Plato

Trains & Things!
Bellissima Publishing, LLC

Introduction

Carson City, Nevada is the capital of Nevada, named after famed mountain man, Kit Carson! The rich, wonderful past of Carson City makes it a fun place for kids to visit, if you know where to look! Here the new mixes with the old, and the old is never forgotten! After the nearby discovery of the Comstock Lode in 1859, Carson City became a thriving commercial center. President Abraham Lincoln, recognizing the importance of Nevada's silver and gold to the Union's Civil War effort, signed a proclamation ushering Nevada into statehood on October 31, 1864! The Virginia & Truckee Railroad was completed between Carson City and Virginia City in 1869. a subject about which you can learn more when you visit Carson City's Railroad Museum!

This fun, 'learn to read' book uses word recognition, and word recognition and rhyme. Written by the award winning author, attorney and former teacher, Penelope Dyan, with photography by John D. Weigand, its extra large print is easy on little eyes. This book is fun with a purpose! To make the learning experience even more exciting, there is a free music video on the Bellissimavideo YouTube Channel that goes along with this book.

Trains & Things!
Bellissima Publishing, LLC

Trains & Things!
A Kid's Guide To Carson City, Nevada

Photography by John D. Weigand
Poetry by Penelope Dyan

There is a Railroad Museum
in Carson City that allows you
to look back to the past,
amd you realize while many things
are now gone,
some things were built to last.

A red wooden caboose was pulled
at the end of the train,
that ran on the railroad tracks
through sleet, snow and rain.
Trains ran from Carson City
to Virgina City,
and then they came back . . .
just a chug, chug, chugging . . .
right down that railroad track.

You see a logging wagon built in 1870 at Bassett Station.
It was used to haul lumber to the Sierra Butte Mines.
Teams of oxen pulled this wagon forward,
tied together into lines.

You imagine traveling down this track,
of looking forward,
as in time you look back.
You remember the Comstock Lode,
and all the stories you've been told,
of how Carson City grew
in so many ways,
many years ago
in the Gold Rush Days.
And because of the finding in Nevada
of silver and gold,
Abraham Lincoln made Nevada a state
to help fund the Civil War,
you are told.

Then you see a birdhouse,
as simple as can be,
sitting right above another birdhouse
atop what used to be a tree.
And you wonder
as you look up into the sky of blue,
if only one family of birds lives here,
or if
(because there's two birdhouses)
of bird families there are two.

And then as you are putting
all of this right into your head,
you spot a wooden water tower!
And it's painted bright, bright red!

Later, you see a windmill,
overlooking a shopping mall,
Mom says,
"This place is beautiful!
And Carson City has it ALL!"

It gets dark, and you are hungry.
You all wonder what to do.
You'd like to eat here,
but this place closed promptly,
right at two!
Your mom says,
"Well, that's awfully early to close."
Your dad sneezes and blows his nose.

You walk right past
the St. Charles Hotel.
It was built way back in 1862.
Your tummy starts to grumble,
because you're hungry
and the day is through.
And then as you walk along,
your parents talk.
And YOU hum a song

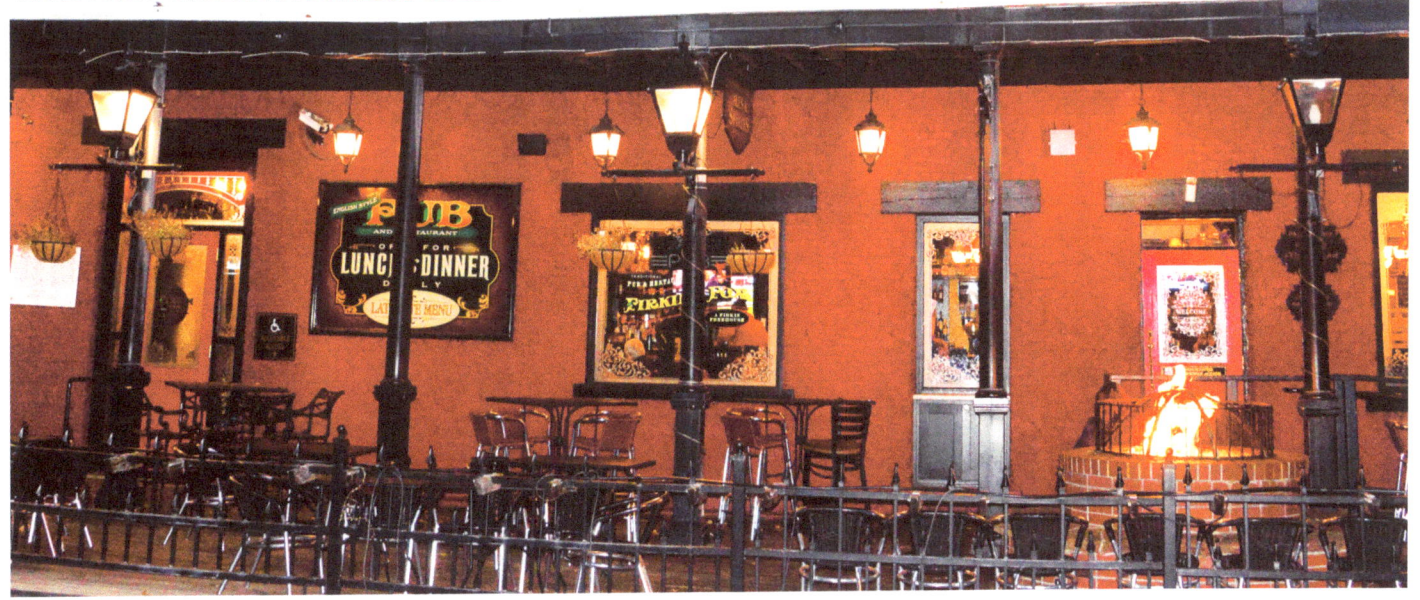

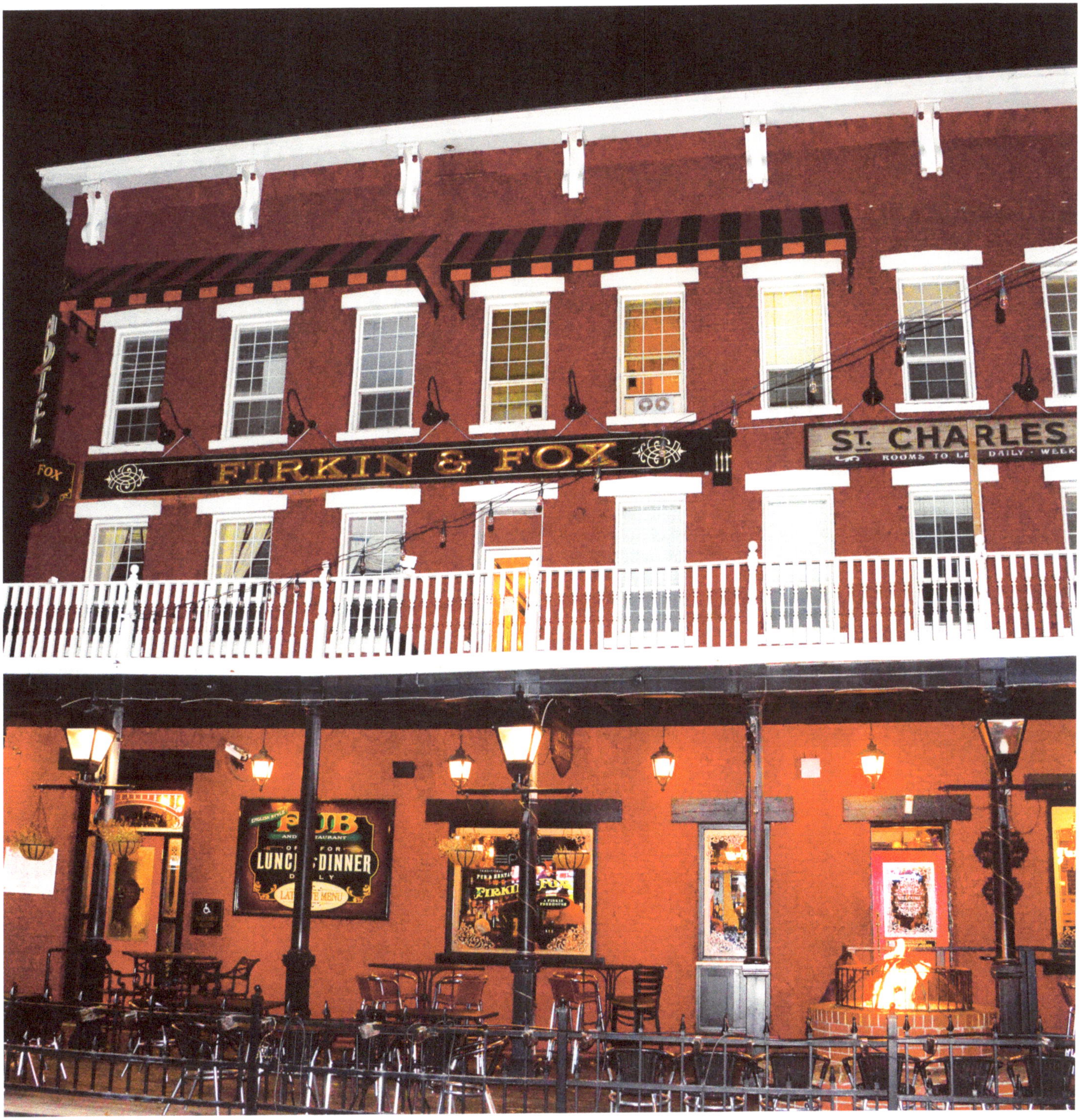
FIRKIN & FOX
ST. CHARLES
ROOMS TO LE
DAILY · WEEK
PUB
AND RESTAURANT
LUNCH
DINNER

Nevada's Attorney General's office
lights the dark of the night,
Because Mom says, "The wheels
of justice depend on this office,"
YOU decide it's ONLY right.
After all, you decide.
justice is supposed to be a beacon,
and a beacon IS a light,
guiding the weary traveler
through darkness into light!
And then those who are lost
are found once again,
as through the perils of life's journey,
they carefully wend.

The great Nevada Territory
was formed in 1861.
But it would be more than
a territory before history was done!
Nevada was granted statehood
on October 31, 1864.
Its gold and its silver
helped fund the Civil War.
In 1870 this Capitol building
was complete,
and here is where
Nevada's governor took his seat.

At last you arrive at
Mom and Pop's Diner,
where the drinks are cold
and the food couldn't be finer!
It has been, after all,
a quite perfect day;
but now it is time
to move along on your way.
Days come and days go,
because days aren't meant to last.
But sometimes . . .
in the blink of an eye . . .
you glimpse of things long past!
And in Carson City's past you can see,
a great big piece of history!

"Let every man be master of his time."

William Shakespeare, Macbeth